BUILDING A 12 KEY FACILITY FOR THE JAZZ BASSIST
Book II

Methods for Practicing Scales, Modes & Arpeggios in 12 keys

Upright
&
Electric Bass
Edition

By Steven Mooney

This book is dedicated to my wife Madoka and my son James Omega Mooney
Special thanks to Jimmy Vass, Darcy Wright and Charlie Banacos.

Inspiration for the book comes from the following words.
   " *there again, get those things down in all 12 keys* "
Darcy Wright.

1st Edition October 2013

Print Edition   ISBN 978-1-937187-22-4
eBook Edition ISBN 978-1-937187-28-6

Library of Congress Control Number: 2013955844
Musical Score : Jazz
Musical Score : Studies & exercises, etudes

Layout and music engraving by Steven Mooney
Cover Design by Steven Mooney

Table of Contents.

Part I MAJOR SCALE studies in 12 keys

Table of Contents.

Part II MELODIC MINOR SCALE studies in 12 keys

Table of contents.

Part III Symmetric scales

Table of contents

Table of contents.

Foreward

Building a 12 key Facility for the Jazz Bassist Pt. II - Methods for practicing scales, modes & arpeggios.

 While Building a 12 key Facility Pt. I Book IV in the "Constructing Walking Jazz Bass Lines " series for the upright & electric bassist focuses on practicing jazz standard and bebop chord progressions in 12 keys, a task practised rigorously by the masters of the jazz idiom.

 Building a 12 key Facility Pt. II Book V in the "Constructing Walking Jazz Bass Lines" series outlines the various approaches used to build instrumental facility through the study of scales, modes and arpeggios.

 Included are the Major and Melodic minor scales, arpeggios and modes in 12 keys, Bebop scales, Blues scales, Major and Minor pentatonic scales and the Harmonic minor scale all in 12 keys.

Also included are the symmetric scales : Whole tone, Diminished & Augmented scales in triad and 7th chord formations.

Incorporating these techniques into the daily practice routine will solidify the core foundational structures required for the improvising musician of all genres.

Scale studies are utilised by the bassist to learn harmony and instrumental facility while building dexterity, flexibilty and stamina.

The 12 key exercise drills in this book are used as an aid to building muscle memory and training the ear.

An excellent resource of information for bass players and music teachers of all levels

Practicing scales and having a dedicated daily practice routine are at the core of professional musicians worldwide.

Part I   Scale studies in the key of C Major

Scales, Modes and Arpeggios over 2 octaves

C Major scale

C maj7 arpeggio

D Dorian scale

D min 7 arpeggio

E Phrygian scale

E min 7 arpeggio

F Lydian scale

F maj 7 arpeggio

G Mixolydian scale

G 7 arpeggio

A Aeolian scale

A min7 arpeggio

B Locrian scale

B min7 b5 arpeggio

4 Note Scale Groupings

The following exercise outlines the use of 4 note groupings moving stepwise diatonically through the scale of C major.

For example, the 4 note grouping starts on the root note or 1st degree of the scale and progresses stepwise. The exercise then descends from the 2nd octave C back to the root.

Ascending

Descending

Permutation 2

Up & Down

As in the previous exercise the following exercise outlines the use of 4 note groupings moving stepwise diatonically through the scale of C major.

Notice in exercise #2 the 4 note grouping starts on the root note or 1st degree of the scale and progresses stepwise. In this example we descend when we hit the 5th note in the sequence eg. descending from the 2nd 4 note grouping.

Ascending

Descending

Broken Thirds

Ascending

Descending

3 Note Groupings

C major scale in triplet groupings
Ascending

Descending

Diatonic 7th Chords in Triplets

C major arpeggio

D min7 arpeggio

E min7 arpeggio

F maj 7 arpeggio

G 7 arpeggio

*The D natural in this exercise is out of the range of the 4 string bass without C extension. This passage can be played 8va eg. 1 octave higher than written.

A min7 arpeggio

B min7 b5 arpeggio

C major arpeggio

4 Note Groupings Diatonic Triads

Ascending 1351

maj   min   min   maj   maj   min   dim   maj

Descending 1351

maj   dim   min   maj   maj   min   min   maj

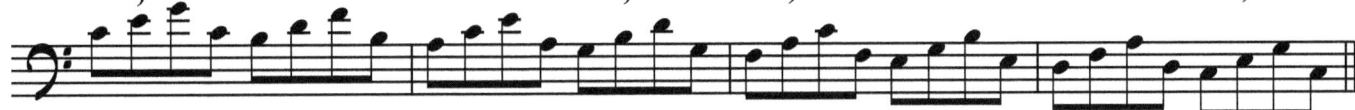

Ascending 1531

maj   min   min   maj   maj   min   dim   maj

Descending 1531

maj   dim   min   maj   maj   min   min   maj

4 Note Groupings Diatonic 7th Chords

Ascending

maj7   min7   min7   maj7   dom7   min7   half dim   maj7

8 va   min7   min7   maj7   dom7   min7   half dim   maj7

Descending

8 va   maj7   half dim   min7   dom7   maj7   min7   min7   maj7

half dim   min7   dom7   maj7   min7   min7   maj7

4 Note Groupings Diatonic 7th Chords

Permutation 2
Ascending & descending

maj7   min7   min7   maj7   dom7   min7   half dim   maj7

half dim   min7   dom7   maj7   min7   min7   maj7

Permutation 3
Down the chord stepwise up the scale

maj7   min7   min7   maj7   dom7   min7   half dim   maj7

maj7   half dim   min7   dom7   maj7   min7   min7   maj7

Scale studies in the key of Db Major

Scales, Modes and Arpeggios over 2 octaves

Db Major scale

Db maj7 arpeggio

Eb Dorian scale

Eb min7 arpeggio

F Phrygian scale

F min7 arpeggio

Gb Lydian scale

Gb maj7 arpeggio

Ab Mixolydian scale

Ab7 arpeggio

Bb Aeolian scale

Bb min7 arpeggio

C Locrian scale

C min7 b5 arpeggio

4 Note Scale Groupings

The following exercise outlines the use of 4 note groupings moving stepwise diatonically through the scale of Db major.

For example, the 4 note grouping starts on the root note or 1st degree of the scale and progresses stepwise. The exercise then descends from the 2nd octave Db back to the root.

Ascending

Descending

Permutation 2   Up & Down

As in the previous exercise the following exercise outlines the use of 4 note groupings moving stepwise diatonically through the scale of Db major.

Notice in exercise #2 the 4 note grouping starts on the root note or 1st degree of the scale and progresses stepwise. In this example we descend when we hit the 5th note in the sequence eg. descending from the 2nd 4 note grouping.

Ascending

Descending

Broken Thirds

Ascending

Descending

3 Note Groupings

Db major scale in triplet groupings
Ascending

Descending

Diatonic 7th Chords in Triplets

Db major arpeggio

Eb min7 arpeggio

F min7 arpeggio

Gb maj 7 arpeggio

Ab 7 arpeggio

*The low Eb in this exercise is out of the range of the 4 string bass without C extension. This passage can be played 8va eg. 1 octave higher than written.

©Waterfall Publishing House 2013

Building a 12 key Facility Pt II

Bb min7 arpeggio

C min7 b5 arpeggio

Db major arpeggio

4 Note Groupings Diatonic Triads

Ascending 1351

maj   min   min   maj   maj   min   dim   maj

Descending 1351

maj   dim   min   maj   maj   min   min   maj

Ascending 1531

maj   min   min   maj   maj   min   dim   maj

Descending 1531

maj   dim   min   maj   maj   min   min   maj

4 Note Groupings Diatonic 7th Chords

Ascending
maj7 min7 min7 maj7 dom7 min7 half dim maj7

8 va min7 min7 maj7 dom7 min7 half dim maj7

Descending
8 va maj7 half dim min7 dom7 maj7 min7 min7 maj7

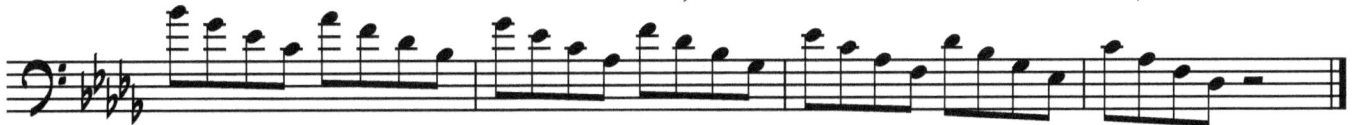

half dim min7 dom7 maj7 min7 min7 maj7

Permutation 2
Ascending & descending
maj7 min7 min7 maj7 dom7 min7 half dim maj7

half dim min7 dom7 maj7 min7 min7 maj7

Permutation 3
Down the chord stepwise up the scale

Scale studies in the key of D Major

Scales, Modes and Arpeggios over 2 octaves

D Major 7 scale

D maj 7 arpeggio

E Dorian scale

E min7 arpeggio

F# Phrygian scale

F# min7 arpeggio

G Lydian scale

G maj 7 arpeggio

A Mixolydian scale

A dom7 arpeggio

B Aeolian scale

B min7 arpeggio

C# Locrian scale

C# min7 b5 arpeggio

4 Note Scale Groupings

The following exercise outlines the use of 4 note groupings moving stepwise diatonically through the scale of D major.

For example, the 4 note grouping starts on the root note or 1st degree of the scale and progresses stepwise. The exercise then descends from the 2nd octave D back to the root.

Ascending

Descending

Permutation 2   Up & Down

As in the previous exercise the following exercise outlines the use of 4 note groupings moving stepwise diatonically through the scale of D major.

Notice in exercise #2 the 4 note grouping starts on the root note or 1st degree of the scale and progresses stepwise. In this example we descend when we hit the 5th note in the sequence eg. descending from the 2nd 4 note grouping.

Ascending

Descending

Broken Thirds

Ascending

Descending

3 Note Groupings

D major scale in triplet groupings
Ascending

Descending

Diatonic 7th Chords in Triplets

D maj arpeggio

E min7 arpeggio

F# min7 arpeggio

G maj 7 arpeggio

A 7 arpeggio

B min7 arpeggio

C# min7 b5 arpeggio

D major arpeggio

4 Note Groupings Diatonic Triads

Ascending 1351

maj min min maj maj min dim maj

Descending 1351

maj dim min maj maj min min maj

Ascending 1531

maj min min maj maj min dim maj

Descending 1531

maj dim min maj maj min min maj

4 Note Groupings Diatonic 7th chords

Ascending

maj7   min7   min7   maj7   dom7   min7   half dim   maj7

8 va   min7   min7   maj7   dom7   min7   half dim   maj7

Descending

8 va   maj7   half dim   min7   dom7   maj7   min7   min7   maj7

half dim   min7   dom7   maj7   min7   min7   maj7

Permutation 2
Ascending & descending

maj7   min7   min7   maj7   dom7   min7   half dim   maj7

half dim   min7   dom7   maj7   min7   min7   maj7

Permutation 3
Down the chord stepwise up the scale

Scale studies in the key of Eb Major

Scales, Modes and Arpeggios over 2 octaves

Eb Major scale

Eb maj 7 arpeggio

F Dorian scale

F min 7 arpeggio

G Phrygian scale

G min 7 arpeggio

Ab Lydian scale

Ab maj 7 arpeggio

Bb Mixolydian scale

Bb7 arpeggio

C Aeolian scale

C min7 arpeggio

D Locrian scale

D min7 b5 arpeggio

4 Note Scale Groupings

The following exercise outlines the use of 4 note groupings moving stepwise diatonically through the scale of Eb major.

For example, the 4 note grouping starts on the root note or 1st degree of the scale and progresses stepwise. The exercise then descends from the 2nd octave Eb back to the root.

Ascending

Descending

Permutation 2 — Up & Down

As in the previous exercise the following exercise outlines the use of 4 note groupings moving stepwise diatonically through the scale of Eb major.

Notice in exercise #2 the 4 note grouping starts on the root note or 1st degree of the scale and progresses stepwise. In this example we descend when we hit the 5th note in the sequence eg. descending from the 2nd 4 note grouping.

Ascending

Descending

Broken Thirds

Ascending

Descending

3 Note Groupings

Eb major scale in triplet groupings
Ascending

Descending

Diatonic 7th Chords in Triplets

Eb maj arpeggio

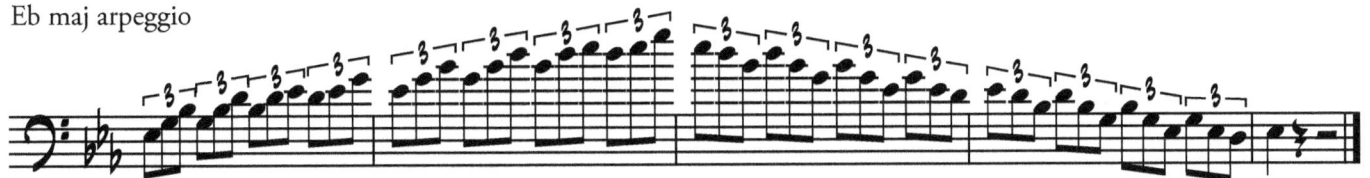

F min7 arpeggio

G min7 arpeggio

Ab maj 7 arpeggio

Bb 7 arpeggio

* The Eb in this exercise is out of the range of the 4 string bass without C extension. This passage can be played 8va eg. 1 octave higher than written.

Building a 12 key Facility Pt II

C min7 arpeggio

D min7 b5 arpeggio

Eb maj arpeggio

4 Note Groupings Diatonic Triads

Ascending 1351

maj   min   min   maj   maj   min   dim   maj

Descending 1351

maj   dim   min   maj   maj   min   min   maj

Ascending 1531

maj   min   min   maj   maj   min   dim   maj

Descending 1531

maj   dim   min   maj   maj   min   min   maj

4 Note Groupings Diatonic 7th Chords

Ascending

maj7 min7 min7 maj7 dom7 min7 half dim maj7

8 va min7 min7 maj7 dom7 min7 half dim maj7

Descending

8 va. maj7 half dim min7 dom7 maj7 min7 min7 maj7

half dim min7 dom7 maj7 min7 min7 maj7

Permutation 2
Ascending & descending

maj7 min7 min7 maj7 dom7 min7 half dim maj7

half dim min7 dom7 maj7 min7 min7 maj7

Building a 12 key Facility Pt II

Permutation 3
Down the chord stepwise up the scale

Scale studies in the key of E Major

Scales, Modes and Arpeggios over 2 octaves

E Major scale

E maj 7 arpeggio

F# Dorian scale

F# min 7 arpeggio

G# Phrygian scale

G# min 7 arpeggio

A Lydian scale

Amaj 7 arpeggio

B Mixolydian scale

B 7 arpeggio

C# Aeolian scale

C# min7 arpeggio

D# Locrian scale

D# min7 b5 arpeggio

4 Note Scale Groupings

The following exercise outlines the use of 4 note groupings moving stepwise diatonically through the scale of E major.

For example, the 4 note grouping starts on the root note or 1st degree of the scale and progresses stepwise. The exercise then descends from the 2nd octave E back to the root.

Ascending

Descending

Permutation 2   Up & Down

As in the previous exercise the following exercise outlines the use of 4 note groupings moving stepwise diatonically through the scale of E major.

Notice in exercise #2 the 4 note grouping starts on the root note or 1st degree of the scale and progresses stepwise. In this example we descend when we hit the 5th note in the sequence eg. descending from the 2nd 4 note grouping.

Ascending

Descending

Broken Thirds

Ascending

Descending

3 Note Groupings

E major scale in triplet groupings
Ascending

Descending

Diatonic 7th Chords in Triplets

E maj arpeggio

F# min7 arpeggio

G# min7 arpeggio

A maj 7 arpeggio

B 7 arpeggio

* The D# in this exercise is out of the range of the 4 string bass without C extension. This passage can be played 8va eg. 1 octave higher than written.

C# min7 arpeggio

D# min7 b5 arpeggio

E maj arpeggio

4 Note Groupings Diatonic Triads

Ascending 1351

maj min min maj maj min dim maj

Descending 1351

maj dim min maj maj min min maj

Ascending 1531

maj min min maj maj min dim maj

Descending 1531

maj dim min maj maj min min maj

4 Note Groupings Diatonic 7th Chords

Ascending

maj7 min7 min7 maj7 dom7 min7 half dim maj7

8 va min7 min7 maj7 dom7 min7 half dim maj7

Descending

8 va maj7 half dim min7 dom7 maj7 min7 min7 maj7

half dim min7 dom7 maj7 min7 min7 maj7

Ascending & descending

maj7 min7 min7 maj7 dom7 min7 half dim maj7

half dim min7 dom7 maj7 min7 min7 maj7

Permutation 3
Down the chord stepwise up the scale

maj7   min7   min7   maj7   dom7   min7   half dim   maj7

maj7   half dim   min7   dom7   maj7   min7   min7   maj7

Scale studies in the key of F Major

Scales, Modes and Arpeggios over 2 octaves

F Major scale

F maj 7 arpeggio

G Dorian scale

G min 7 arpeggio

A Phrygian scale

A min 7 arpeggio

Bb Lydian scale

Bb maj 7 arpeggio

C Mixolydian scale

C 7 arpeggio

D Aeolian scale

D min7 arpeggio

E Locrian scale

E min7 b5 arpeggio

4 Note Scale Groupings

The following exercise outlines the use of 4 note groupings moving stepwise diatonically through the scale of F major.

For example, the 4 note grouping starts on the root note or 1st degree of the scale and progresses stepwise. The exercise then descends from the 2nd octave F back to the root.

Ascending

Descending

*The D in this exercise is out of the range of the 4 string bass without C extension. This passage can be played 8va eg. 1 octave higher than written.

Permutation 2   Up & Down

As in the previous exercise the following exercise outlines the use of 4 note groupings moving stepwise diatonically through the scale of F major.

Notice in exercise #2 the 4 note grouping starts on the root note or 1st degree of the scale and progresses stepwise. In this example we descend when we hit the 5th note in the sequence eg. descending from the 2nd 4 note grouping.

Ascending

Descending

Broken Thirds

Ascending

Descending

3 Note Groupings

F major scale in triplet groupings
Ascending

Descending

Diatonic 7th Chords in Triplets

F maj arpeggio

G min7 arpeggio

A min7 arpeggio

Bb maj 7 arpeggio

C 7 arpeggio

Building a 12 key Facility Pt II

D min7 arpeggio

E min7 b5 arpeggio

F major arpeggio

4 Note Groupings Diatonic Triads

Ascending 1351

maj   min   min   maj   maj   min   dim   maj

Descending 1351

maj   dim   min   maj   maj   min   min   maj

Ascending 1531

maj   min   min   maj   maj   min   dim   maj

Descending 1531

maj   dim   min   maj   maj   min   min   maj

4 Note Groupings Diatonic 7th Chords

Ascending

maj7 min7 min7 maj7 dom7 min7 half dim maj7

8 va min7 min7 maj7 dom7 min7 half dim maj7

Descending

8 va maj7 half dim min7 dom7 maj7 min7 min7 maj7

half dim min7 dom7 maj7 min7 min7 maj7

Permutation 2
Ascending & descending

maj7 min7 min7 maj7 dom7 min7 half dim maj7

half dim min7 dom7 maj7 min7 min7 maj7

Building a 12 key Facility Pt II

Permutation 3
Down the chord stepwise up the scale

Scale studies in the key of F# Major

Scales, Modes and Arpeggios over 2 octaves

F# Major scale

F# maj 7 arpeggio

G# Dorian scale

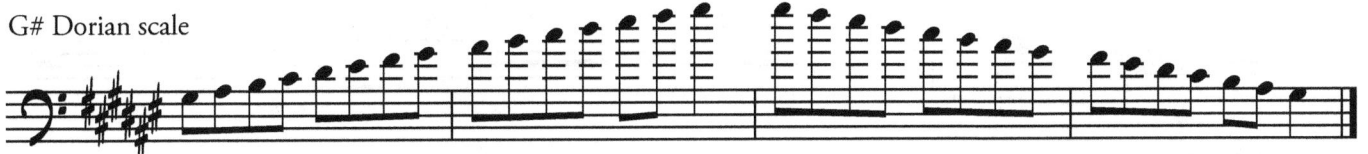

G# min 7 arpeggio

A# Phrygian scale

A# min 7 arpeggio

B Lydian scale

B major 7 arpeggio

Building a 12 key Facility Pt II

C# Mixolydian scale

C# 7 arpeggio

D# Aeolian scale

D# min7 arpeggio

E# Locrian scale

E# min7 b5 arpeggio

4 Note Scale Groupings

The following exercise outlines the use of 4 note groupings moving stepwise diatonically through the scale of F# major.

For example, the 4 note grouping starts on the root note or 1st degree of the scale and progresses stepwise. The exercise then descends from the 2nd octave F# back to the root.

Ascending

Descending

* The D# in this exercise is out of the range of the 4 string bass without C extension. This passage can
be played 8va eg. 1 octave higher than written.

Permutation 2   Up & Down

As in the previous exercise the following exercise outlines the use of 4 note groupings moving stepwise
diatonically through the scale of F# major.

Notice in exercise #2 the 4 note grouping starts on the root note or 1st degree of the scale and progresses
stepwise. In this example we descend when we hit the 5th note in the sequence eg. descending from the
2nd 4 note grouping.

Ascending

Descending

Broken Thirds

Ascending

Descending

©Waterfall Publishing House 2013

3 Note Groupings

F# major scale in triplet groupings
Ascending

Descending

Diatonic 7th Chords in Ttriplets

F# maj arpeggio

G# min7 arpeggio

A# min7 arpeggio

B maj 7 arpeggio

C# 7 arpeggio

D# min7 arpeggio

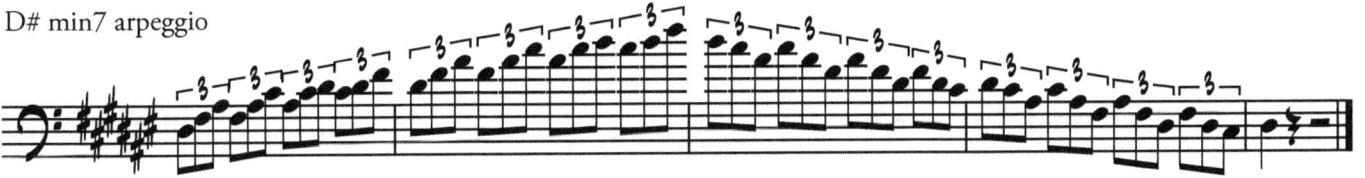

E# min7 b5 arpeggio

F# maj arpeggio

4 Note Groupings Diatonic Triads

Ascending 1351

maj   min   min   maj   maj   min   dim   maj

Descending 1351

maj   dim   min   maj   maj   min   min   maj

Ascending 1531

maj   min   min   maj   maj   min   dim   maj

Descending 1531

maj   dim   min   maj   maj   min   min   maj

* The D# in this exercise is out of the range of the 4 string bass without C extension. This passage can be played 8va eg. 1 octave higher than written.

4 Note Groupings Diatonic 7th Chords

Ascending

maj7   min7   min7   maj7   dom7   min7   half dim   maj7

8 va   min7   min7   maj7   dom7   min7   half dim   maj7

Descending

8 va   maj7   half dim   min7   dom7   maj7   min7   min7   maj7

half dim   min7   dom7   maj7   min7   min7   maj7

Permutation 2
Ascending & descending

maj7   min7   min7   maj7   dom7   min7   half dim   maj7

half dim   min7   dom7   maj7   min7   min7   maj7

Permutation 3
Down the chord stepwise up the scale

maj7   min7   min7   maj7   dom7   min7   half dim   maj7

maj7   half dim   min7   dom7   maj7   min7   min7   maj7

Scale studies in the key of G Major

Scales, Modes and Arpeggios over 2 octaves

G Major scale

G maj 7 arpeggio

A Dorian scale

A min 7 arpeggio

B Phrygian scale

B min 7 arpeggio

C Lydian scale

C maj 7 arpeggio

D Mixolydian scale

D 7 arpeggio

E Aeolian scale

E min7 arpeggio

F# Locrian scale

F# min7 b5 arpeggio

4 Note Scale Groupings

The following exercise outlines the use of 4 note groupings moving stepwise diatonically through the scale of G major.

For example, the 4 note grouping starts on the root note or 1st degree of the scale and progresses stepwise. The exercise then descends from the 2nd octave G back to the root.

Ascending

Descending

Permutation 2

Up & Down

As in the previous exercise the following exercise outlines the use of 4 note groupings moving stepwise diatonically through the scale of G major.

Notice in exercise #2 the 4 note grouping starts on the root note or 1st degree of the scale and progresses stepwise. In this example we descend when we hit the 5th note in the sequence eg. descending from the 2nd 4 note grouping.

Ascending

Descending

Broken Thirds

Ascending

Descending

3 Note Groupings

G major scale in triplet groupings
Ascending

Descending

Diatonic 7th Chords in Triplets

G Maj arpeggio

A min7 arpeggio

B min7 arpeggio

C maj 7 arpeggio

D 7 arpeggio

Building a 12 key Facility Pt II

E min7 arpeggio

F# min7 b5 arpeggio

G major arpeggio

4 Note Groupings Diatonic Triads

Ascending 1351

maj   min   min   maj   maj   min   dim   maj

Descending 1351

maj   dim   min   maj   maj   min   min   maj

Ascending 1531

maj   min   min   maj   maj   min   dim   maj

Descending 1531

maj   dim   min   maj   maj   min   min   maj

4 Note Groupings Diatonic 7th Chords

Ascending

maj7 min7 min7 maj7 dom7 min7 half dim maj7

8 va min7 min7 maj7 dom7 min7 half dim maj7

Descending

8 va maj7 half dim min7 dom7 maj7 min7 min7 maj7

half dim min7 dom7 maj7 min7 min7 maj7

Permutation 2
Ascending & descending

maj7 min7 min7 maj7 dom7 min7 half dim maj7

half dim min7 dom7 maj7 min7 min7 maj7

Building a 12 key Facility Pt II

Permutation 3
Down the chord stepwise up the scale

Scale studies in the key of Ab Major

Scales, Modes and Arpeggios over 2 octaves

Ab Major scale

Ab maj 7 arpeggio

Bb Dorian scale

Bb min 7 arpeggio

C Phrygian scale

C min 7 arpeggio

Db Lydian scale

Db maj 7 arpeggio

Building a 12 key Facility Pt II

Eb Mixolydian scale

Eb 7 arpeggio

F Aeolian scale

F min7 arpeggio

G Locrian scale

G min7 b5 arpeggio

4 Note Scale Groupings

The following exercise outlines the use of 4 note groupings moving stepwise diatonically through the scale of Ab major.

For example, the 4 note grouping starts on the root note or 1st degree of the scale and progresses stepwise. The exercise then descends from the 2nd octave Ab back to the root.

Ascending

Descending

Permutation 2   Up & Down

As in the previous exercise the following exercise outlines the use of 4 note groupings moving stepwise diatonically through the scale of Ab major.

Notice in exercise #2 the 4 note grouping starts on the root note or 1st degree of the scale and progresses stepwise. In this example we descend when we hit the 5th note in the sequence eg. descending from the 2nd 4 note grouping.

Ascending

Descending

Broken Thirds

Ascending

Descending

3 Note Groupings

Ab major scale in triplet groupings
Ascending

Descending

Diatonic 7th Chords in Triplets

Ab maj arpeggio

Bb min7 arpeggio

C min7 arpeggio

Db maj 7 arpeggio

Eb 7 arpeggio

F min7 arpeggio

G min7 b5 arpeggio

Ab maj arpeggio

4 Note Groupings Diatonic Triads

Ascending 1351

maj min min maj maj min dim maj

Descending 1351

maj dim min maj maj min min maj

Ascending 1531

maj min min maj maj min dim maj

Descending 1531

maj dim min maj maj min min maj

4 Note Groupings Diatonic 7th Chords

Ascending

maj7　min7　min7　maj7　dom7　min7　half dim　maj7

8 va　min7　min7　maj7　dom7　min7　half dim　maj7

Descending

8 va　maj7　half dim　min7　dom7　maj7　min7　min7　maj7

half dim　min7　dom7　maj7　min7　min7　maj7

Permutation 2
Ascending & descending

maj7　min7　min7　maj7　dom7　min7　half dim　maj7

half dim　min7　dom7　maj7　min7　min7　maj7

Permutation 3
Down the chord stepwise up the scale

Scale studies in the key of A Major

Scales, Modes and Arpeggios over 2 octaves

A Major scale

A maj 7 arpeggio

B Dorian scale

B min 7 arpeggio

C# Phrygian scale

C# min 7 arpeggio

D Lydian scale

D maj 7 arpeggio

E Mixolydian scale

E 7 arpeggio

F# Aeolian scale

F# min7 arpeggio

G# Locrian scale

G# min7 b5 arpeggio

4 Note Scale Groupings

The following exercise outlines the use of 4 note groupings moving stepwise diatonically through the scale of A major.

For example, the 4 note grouping starts on the root note or 1st degree of the scale and progresses stepwise. The exercise then descends from the 2nd octave A back to the root.

Ascending

Descending

Permutation 2   Up & Down

As in the previous exercise the following exercise outlines the use of 4 note groupings moving stepwise diatonically through the scale of A major.

Notice in exercise #2 the 4 note grouping starts on the root note or 1st degree of the scale and progresses stepwise. In this example we descend when we hit the 5th note in the sequence eg. descending from the 2nd 4 note grouping.

Ascending

Descending

Broken Thirds

Ascending

Descending

3 Note Groupings

A major scale in triplet groupings
Ascending

Descending

Diatonic 7th Chords in Triplets

A maj arpeggio

B min7 arpeggio

C# min7 arpeggio

D maj 7 arpeggio

E 7 arpeggio

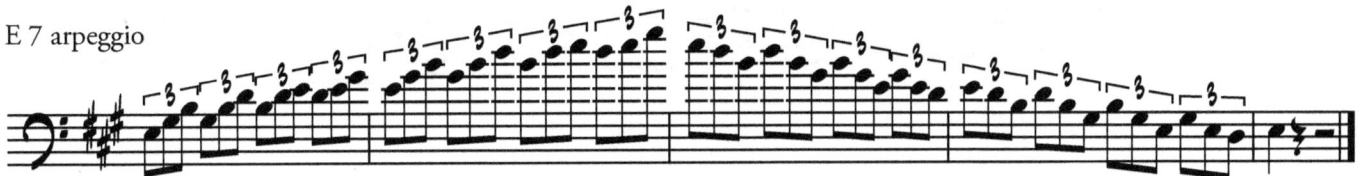

Building a 12 key Facility Pt II

F# min7 arpeggio

A maj arpeggio

G# min7 b5 arpeggio

A maj arpeggio

4 Note Groupings Diatonic Triads

Ascending 1351

maj   min   min   maj   maj   min   dim   maj

Descending 1351

maj   dim   min   maj   maj   min   min   maj

Ascending 1531

maj   min   min   maj   maj   min   dim   maj

Descending 1531

maj   dim   min   maj   maj   min   min   maj

4 Note Groupings Diatonic 7th Chords

Ascending

maj7   min7   min7   maj7   dom7   min7   half dim   maj7

8 va   min7   min7   maj7   dom7   min7   half dim   maj7

Descending

8 va   maj7   half dim   min7   dom7   maj7   min7   min7   maj7

half dim   min7   dom7   maj7   min7   min7   maj7

Permutation 2
Ascending & descending

maj7   min7   min7   maj7   dom7   min7   half dim   maj7

half dim   min7   dom7   maj7   min7   min7   maj7

Permutation 3
Down the chord stepwise up the scale

Scale studies in the key of Bb Major

Scales, Modes and Arpeggios over 2 octaves

Bb Major scale

Bb maj 7 arpeggio

C Dorian scale

C min 7 arpeggio

D Phrygian scale

D min 7 arpeggio

Eb Lydian scale

Eb maj 7 arpeggio

Building a 12 key Facility Pt II

F Mixolydian scale

F 7 arpeggio

G Aeolian scale

G min7 arpeggio

A Locrian scale

A min7 b5 arpeggio

4 Note Scale Groupings

The following exercise outlines the use of 4 note groupings moving stepwise diatonically through the scale of Bb major.

For example, the 4 note grouping starts on the root note or 1st degree of the scale and progresses stepwise. The exercise then descends from the 2nd octave Bb back to the root.

Ascending

Descending

Permutation 2

Up & Down

As in the previous exercise the following exercise outlines the use of 4 note groupings moving stepwise diatonically through the scale of Bb major.

Notice in exercise #2 the 4 note grouping starts on the root note or 1st degree of the scale and progresses stepwise. In this example we descend when we hit the 5th note in the sequence eg. descending from the 2nd 4 note grouping.

Ascending

Descending

Broken Thirds

Ascending

Descending

3 Note Groupings

Bb major scale in triplet groupings
Ascending

Descending

Diatonic 7th Chords in Triplets

Bb maj arpeggio

C min7 arpeggio

D min7 arpeggio

Eb maj 7 arpeggio

F 7 arpeggio

G min7 arpeggio

A min7 b5 arpeggio

Bb major arpeggio

4 Note Groupings Diatonic Triads

Ascending 1351

maj   min   min   maj   maj   min   dim   maj

Descending 1351

maj   dim   min   maj   maj   min   min   maj

Ascending 1531

maj   min   min   maj   maj   min   dim   maj

Descending 1531

maj   dim   min   maj   maj   min   min   maj

4 Note Groupings Diatonic 7th Chords

Ascending

maj7   min7   min7   maj7   dom7   min7   half dim   maj7

8 va   min7   min7   maj7   dom7   min7   half dim   maj7

Descending

8 va   maj7   half dim   min7   dom7   maj7   min7   min7   maj7

half dim   min7   dom7   maj7   min7   min7   maj7

Permutation 2
Ascending & descending

maj7   min7   min7   maj7   dom7   min7   half dim   maj7

half dim   min7   dom7   maj7   min7   min7   maj7

Permutation 3
Down the chord stepwise up the scale

maj7   min7   min7   maj7   dom7   min7   half dim   maj7

maj7   half dim   min7   dom7   maj7   min7   min7   maj7

Scale studies in the key of B Major

Scales, Modes and Arpeggios over 2 octaves

B Major scale

B maj 7 arpeggio

C# Dorian scale

C# min 7 arpeggio

D# Phrygian scale

D# min 7 arpeggio

E Lydian scale

E maj 7 arpeggio

F# Mixolydian scale

F# 7 arpeggio

G# Aeolian scale

G# min7 arpeggio

A# Locrian scale

A# min7 b5 arpeggio

4 Note Scale Groupings

The following exercise outlines the use of 4 note groupings moving stepwise diatonically through the scale of B major.

For example, the 4 note grouping starts on the root note or 1st degree of the scale and progresses stepwise. The exercise then descends from the 2nd octave B back to the root.

Ascending

Descending

Permutation 2   Up & Down

As in the previous exercise the following exercise outlines the use of 4 note groupings moving stepwise diatonically through the scale of B major.

Notice in exercise #2 the 4 note grouping starts on the root note or 1st degree of the scale and progresses stepwise. In this example we descend when we hit the 5th note in the sequence eg. descending from the 2nd 4 note grouping.

Ascending

Descending

Broken Thirds

Ascending

Descending

3 Note Groupings

B major scale in triplet groupings
Ascending

Descending

Diatonic 7th Chords in Triplets

B maj arpeggio

C# min7 arpeggio

D# min7 arpeggio

E maj 7 arpeggio

F# 7 arpeggio

Building a 12 key Facility Pt II

G# min7 arpeggio

A# min7 b5 arpeggio

B maj arpeggio

4 Note Groupings Diatonic Triads

Ascending 1351

maj   min   min   maj   maj   min   dim   maj

Descending 1351

maj   dim   min   maj   maj   min   min   maj

Ascending 1531

maj   min   min   maj   maj   min   dim   maj

Descending 1531

maj   dim   min   maj   maj   min   min   maj

4 Note Groupings Diatonic 7th Chords

Ascending

maj7   min7   min7   maj7   dom7   min7   half dim   maj7

8 va   min7   min7   maj7   dom7   min7   half dim   maj7

Descending

8 va   maj7   half dim   min7   dom7   maj7   min7   min7   maj7

half dim   min7   dom7   maj7   min7   min7   maj7

Permutation 2
Ascending & descending

maj7   min7   min7   maj7   dom7   min7   half dim   maj7

half dim   min7   dom7   maj7   min7   min7   maj7

Permutation 3
Down the chord stepwise up the scale

maj7   min7   min7   maj7   dom7   min7   half dim   maj7

maj7   half dim   min7   dom7   maj7   min7   min7   maj7

Part II   Scale studies in the key of C Melodic Minor (Ascending)

Scales, Modes and Arpeggios over 2 octaves

C Melodic minor scale

C min maj7 arpeggio

D sus b9 scale

D min7 arpeggio * *

Eb Lydian augmented scale

Eb maj #5 arpeggio

F Lydian dominant scale

F 7 #11 arpeggio

* For the purpose of this book we will be using the ascending melodic minor scale also known as the " jazz minor scale ". The melodic minor scale uses a different interval structure when descending when used in classical music.

** Shown here are the " diatonic " 7th chords built from the scale eg min 7th and not a Sus b9 arpeggio.

Building a 12 key Facility Pt II

C Melodic minor/G scale

G7 arpeggio

A Locrian #2 scale

A min7 b5 arpeggio

B Altered scale

B Alt. arpeggio

4 Note Scale Groupings

The following exercise outlines the use of 4 note groupings moving stepwise diatonically through the scale of C melodic minor

For example, the 4 note grouping starts on the root note or 1st degree of the scale and progresses stepwise. The exercise then descends from the 2nd octave C back to the root.

Ascending

Descending

Permutation 2

Up & Down

As in the previous exercise the following exercise outlines the use of 4 note groupings moving stepwise diatonically through the scale of C melodic minor.

Notice in exercise #2 the 4 note grouping starts on the root note or 1st degree of the scale and progresses stepwise. In this example we descend when we hit the 5th note in the sequence eg. descending from the 2nd 4 note grouping.

Ascending

Descending

Broken Thirds

Ascending

Descending

3 Note Groupings

C Melodic minor scale in triplet groupings
Ascending

Descending

Diatonic 7th Chords in Triplets

Starting on the Root
C min/maj7 arpeggio

Starting on the 2nd
D min7 arpeggio

Starting on the 3rd
Eb maj7/#5 arpeggio

Starting on the 4th
F 7#11 arpeggio

Starting on the 5th
G7 arpeggio

Starting on the 6th
A min7b5 arpeggio

Starting on the 7th
B min7 b5 arpeggio

Starting on the Root
C min/maj7 arpeggio

4 Note Groupings Diatonic Triads

Ascending 1351

min   min   aug   maj   maj   dim   dim   min

Descending 1351

min   dim   dim   maj   maj   aug   min   min

Ascending 1531

min   min   aug   maj   maj   dim   dim   min

Descending 1531

min   dim   dim   maj   maj   aug   min   min

4 Note Groupings Diatonic 7th Chords

Ascending

Descending

Permutation 2
Ascending & descending

Permutation 3
Down the chord stepwise up the scale

min/maj7 min7   maj7#5   dom7   dom7   half dim7   half dim7   min/maj7

min/maj7   half dim7   half dim7   dom7   dom7   maj7 #5   min7   min/maj7

Scale studies in the key of C# Melodic Minor

Scales, Modes and Arpeggios over 2 octaves

C# Melodic minor scale

C# min maj7 arpeggio

D# sus b9 scale

D# sus b9 arpeggio

E Lydian augmented scale

E maj #5 arpeggio

F# Lydian dominant scale

F# 7 #11 arpeggio

C# Melodic minor/G# scale

C# minmaj7 /G# arpeggio

A# Locrian #2 scale

A# min7 b5 arpeggio

B# Altered scale

B# Alt. arpeggio

4 Note Scale Groupings

The following exercise outlines the use of 4 note groupings moving stepwise diatonically through the scale of C# melodic minor.

For example, the 4 note grouping starts on the root note or 1st degree of the scale and progresses stepwise . The exercise then descends from the 2nd octave C# back to the root.

Ascending

Descending

Permutation 2   Up & Down

As in the previous exercise the following exercise outlines the use of 4 note groupings moving stepwise diatonically through the scale of C# melodic minor.

Notice in exercise #2 the 4 note grouping starts on the root note or 1st degree of the scale and progresses stepwise. In this example we descend when we hit the 5th note in the sequence eg. descending from the 2nd 4 note grouping.

Ascending

Descending

Broken Thirds

Ascending

Descending

3 Note Groupings

C # Melodic minor scale in triplet groupings
Ascending

Descending

Diatonic 7th Chords in Triplets

Starting on the Root
C# min/maj7 arpeggio

Starting on the 2nd
D# min7 arpeggio

Starting on the 3rd
E maj7/#5 arpeggio

Starting on the 4th
F# 7#11 arpeggio

Starting on the 5th
G# 7 arpeggio

Building a 12 key Facility Pt II

Starting on the 6th
A# min7b5 arpeggio

Starting on the 7th
B# min7 b5 arpeggio

Starting on the Root
C# min/maj7 arpeggio

4 Note Groupings Diatonic Triads

Ascending 1351

min   min   aug   maj   maj   dim   dim   min

Descending 1351

min   dim   dim   maj   maj   aug   min   min

Ascending 1531

min   min   aug   maj   maj   dim   dim   min

Descending 1531

min   dim   dim   maj   maj   aug   min   min

4 Note Groupings Diatonic 7th Chords

Ascending

min/maj7 min7   maj7#5   dom7   dom7   half dim7   half dim7 min/maj7

min7   maj7#5   dom7   dom7   half dim7   half dim7   min/maj7

Descending

min/maj7 half dim7 half dim7 dom7   dom7   maj7 #5   min7   min/maj7

half dim7 half dim7 dom7   dom7   maj7 #5   min7   min/maj7

Permutation 2
Ascending & descending

min/maj7 min7   maj7#5   dom7   dom7   half dim7   half dim7 min/maj7

half dim7 half dim7 dom7   dom7   maj7#5   min7   min/maj7

Permutation 3
Down the chord stepwise up the scale

Scale studies in the key of D Melodic Minor

Scales, Modes and Arpeggios over 2 octaves

D Melodic minor scale

D min maj7 arpeggio

E sus b9 scale

E sus b9 arpeggio

F Lydian augmented scale

F maj #5 arpeggio

G Lydian dominant scale

G 7 #11 arpeggio

Building a 12 key Facility Pt II

D Melodic minor/A scale

D minmaj7 /A arpeggio

B Locrian #2 scale

B min7 b5 arpeggio

C# Altered scale

C# Alt. arpeggio

4 Note Scale Groupings

The following exercise outlines the use of 4 note groupings moving stepwise diatonically through the scale of D melodic minor.

For example, the 4 note grouping starts on the root note or 1st degree of the scale and progresses stepwise . The exercise then descends from the 2nd octave D back to the root.

Ascending

Descending

Permutation 2   **Up & Down**

As in the previous exercise the following exercise outlines the use of 4 note groupings moving stepwise diatonically through the scale of D melodic minor.

Notice in exercise #2 the 4 note grouping starts on the root note or 1st degree of the scale and progresses stepwise. In this example we descend when we hit the 5th note in the sequence eg. descending from the 2nd 4 note grouping.

Ascending

Descending

Broken Thirds

Ascending

Descending

3 Note Groupings

D Melodic minor scale in triplet groupings
Ascending

Descending

Diatonic 7th Chords in Triplets

Starting on the Root
D min/maj7 arpeggio

Starting on the 2nd
E min7 arpeggio

Starting on the 3rd
F maj7/#5 arpeggio

Starting on the 4th
G 7#11 arpeggio

Starting on the 5th
A7 arpeggio

Starting on the 6th
B min7 b5 arpeggio

Starting on the 7th
C# min7 b5 arpeggio

Starting on the Root
D min/maj 7 arpeggio

4 Note Grouping Diatonic Triads

Ascending 1351

min   min   aug   maj   maj   dim   dim   min

Descending 1351

min   dim   dim   maj   maj   aug   min   min

Ascending 1531

min   min   aug   maj   maj   dim   dim   min

Descending 1531

min   dim   dim   maj   maj   aug   min   min

4 Note Groupings Diatonic 7th Chords

Ascending

min/maj7 min7   maj7#5   dom7   dom7   half dim7   half dim7   min/maj7

min7   maj7#5   dom7   dom7   half dim7   half dim7   min/maj7

Descending

min/maj7   half dim7   half dim7   dom7   dom7   maj7 #5   min7   min/maj7

half dim7   half dim7   dom7   dom7   maj7 #5   min7   min/maj7

Permutation 2
Ascending & descending

min/maj7 min7   maj7#5   dom7   dom7   half dim7   half dim7   min/maj7

half dim7   half dim7   dom7   dom7   maj7#5   min7   min/maj7

Permutation 3
Down the chord stepwise up the scale

min/maj7 min7   maj7#5   dom7   dom7   half dim7   half dim7   min/maj7

min/maj7 half dim7   half dim7 dom7   dom7   maj7 #5   min7   min/maj7

Scale studies in the key of Eb Melodic Minor

Scales, Modes and Arpeggios over 2 octaves

Eb Melodic minor scale

Eb min maj7 arpeggio

F sus b9 scale

F sus b9 arpeggio

Gb Lydian augmented scale

Gb maj #5 arpeggio

Ab Lydian dominant scale

Ab7 #11 arpeggio

Eb Melodic minor/Bb scale

Eb minmaj7 /Bb arpeggio

C Locrian #2 scale

C min7 b5 arpeggio

D Altered scale

D Alt. arpeggio

4 Note Scale Groupings

The following exercise outlines the use of 4 note groupings moving stepwise diatonically through the scale of Eb melodic minor.

For example, the 4 note grouping starts on the root note or 1st degree of the scale and progresses stepwise . The exercise then descends from the 2nd octave Eb back to the root.

Ascending

Descending

Permutation 2   Up & Down

As in the previous exercise the following exercise outlines the use of 4 note groupings moving stepwise diatonically through the scale of Eb melodic minor.

Notice in exercise #2 the 4 note grouping starts on the root note or 1st degree of the scale and progresses stepwise. In this example we descend when we hit the 5th note in the sequence eg. descending from the 2nd 4 note grouping.

Ascending

Descending

Broken Thirds

Ascending

Descending

3 Note Groupings

Eb Melodic minor scale in triplet groupings
Ascending

Descending

Diatonic 7th Chords in Triplets

Starting on the Root
Eb min/maj7 arpeggio

Starting on the 2nd
F min7 arpeggio

Starting on the 3rd
Gb maj7/#5 arpeggio

Starting on the 4th
Ab 7#11 arpeggio

Starting on the 5th
Bb7 arpeggio

Building a 12 key Facility Pt II

Starting on the 6th
C min7 b5 arpeggio

Starting on the 7th
D min7 b5 arpeggio

Starting on the Root
Eb min/maj 7 arpeggio

4 Note Groupings Diatonic Triads

Ascending 1351

min   min   aug   maj   maj   dim   dim   min

Descending 1351

min   dim   dim   maj   maj   aug   min   min

Ascending 1531

min   min   aug   maj   maj   dim   dim   min

Descending 1531

min   dim   dim   maj   maj   aug   min   min

4 Note Groupings Diatonic 7th Chords

Ascending

min/maj7 min7   maj7#5   dom7   dom7   half dim7   half dim7   min/maj7

min7   maj7#5   dom7   dom7   half dim7   half dim7   min/maj7

Descending

min/maj7   half dim7   half dim7   dom7   dom7   maj7 #5   min7   min/maj7

half dim7   half dim7   dom7   dom7   maj7 #5   min7   min/maj7

Permutation 2
Ascending & descending

min/maj7 min7   maj7#5   dom7   dom7   half dim7   half dim7   min/maj7

half dim7   half dim7   dom7   dom7   maj7#5   min7   min/maj7

Permutation 3
Down the chord stepwise up the scale

min/maj7 min7   maj7#5   dom7   dom7   half dim7   half dim7 min/maj7

min/maj7 half dim7   half dim7 dom7   dom7   maj7 #5   min7   min/maj7

Scale studies in the key of E Melodic Minor

Scales, Modes and Arpeggios over 2 octaves

E Melodic minor scale

E min maj 7 arpeggio

F# sus b9 scale

F# sus b9 arpeggio

G Lydian augmented scale

G maj #5 arpeggio

A Lydian dominant scale

A 7 #11 arpeggio

E Melodic minor/B scale

E minmaj7 / B arpeggio

C# Locrian #2 scale

C# min7 b5 arpeggio

D# Altered scale

D# Alt. arpeggio

4 Note Scale Groupings

The following exercise outlines the use of 4 note groupings moving stepwise diatonically through the scale of E melodic minor.

For example, the 4 note grouping starts on the root note or 1st degree of the scale and progresses stepwise . The exercise then descends from the 2nd octave E back to the root.

Ascending

Descending

Permutation 2   Up & Down

As in the previous exercise the following exercise outlines the use of 4 note groupings moving stepwise diatonically through the scale of E melodic minor.

Notice in exercise #2 the 4 note grouping starts on the root note or 1st degree of the scale and progresses stepwise. In this example we descend when we hit the 5th note in the sequence eg. descending from the 2nd 4 note grouping.

Ascending

Descending

Broken Thirds

Ascending

Descending

3 Note Groupings

E Melodic minor scale in triplet groupings
Ascending

Descending

Diatonic 7th Chords in Triplets

Starting on the Root
E min/maj7 arpeggio

Starting on the 2nd
F# min7 arpeggio

Starting on the 3rd
G maj7/#5 arpeggio

Starting on the 4th
A 7#11 arpeggio

Starting on the 5th
B 7 arpeggio

* The D# in this exercise is out of the range of the 4 string bass without C extension. This passage can be played 8va eg. 1 octave higher than written.

Starting on the 6th
C# min7 b5 arpeggio

Starting on the 7th
D# min7 b5 arpeggio

Starting on the Root
E min/maj 7 arpeggio

4 Note Groupings Diatonic Triads

Ascending 1351

min min aug maj maj dim dim min

Descending 1351

min dim dim maj maj aug min min

Ascending 1531

min min aug maj maj dim dim min

Descending 1531

min dim dim maj maj aug min min

4 Note Groupings Diatonic 7th Chords

Ascending

min/maj7 min7   maj7#5   dom7   dom7   half dim7   half dim7   min/maj7

min7   maj7#5   dom7   dom7   half dim7   half dim7   min/maj7

Descending

min/maj7 half dim7 half dim7 dom7   dom7   maj7 #5   min7   min/maj7

half dim7 half dim7 dom7   dom7   maj7 #5   min7   min/maj7

Permutation 2
Ascending & descending

min/maj7 min7   maj7#5   dom7   dom7   half dim7   half dim7   min/maj7

half dim7 half dim7 dom7   dom7   maj7#5   min7   min/maj7

Permutation 3
Down the chord stepwise up the scale

min/maj7 min7   maj7#5   dom7   dom7   half dim7   half dim7   min/maj

min/maj7   half dim7   half dim7   dom7   dom7   maj7 #5   min7   min/maj7

Scale studies in the key of F Melodic Minor

Scales, Modes and Arpeggios over 2 octaves

F Melodic minor scale

F min maj7 arpeggio

G sus b9 scale

G sus b9 arpeggio

Ab Lydian augmented scale

Ab maj #5 arpeggio

Bb Lydian dominant scale

Bb 7 #11 arpeggio

F Melodic minor/ C scale

F minmaj7 / C arpeggio

D Locrian #2 scale

D min7 b5 arpeggio

E Altered scale

E Alt. arpeggio

4 Note Scale Groupings

The following exercise outlines the use of 4 note groupings moving stepwise diatonically through the scale of F melodic minor.

For example, the 4 note grouping starts on the root note or 1st degree of the scale and progresses stepwise . The exercise then descends from the 2nd octave F back to the root.

Ascending

Descending

*The D in this exercise is out of the range of the 4 string bass without C extension. This passage can be played 8va eg. 1 octave higher than written.

Permutation 2   Up & Down

As in the previous exercise the following exercise outlines the use of 4 note groupings moving stepwise diatonically through the scale of F melodic minor.

Notice in exercise #2 the 4 note grouping starts on the root note or 1st degree of the scale and progresses stepwise. In this example we descend when we hit the 5th note in the sequence eg. descending from the 2nd 4 note grouping.

Ascending

Descending

Broken Thirds

Ascending

Descending

3 Note Groupings

F Melodic minor scale in triplet groupings
Ascending

Descending

*The Eb in this exercise is out of the range of the 4 string bass without C extension. This passage can be played 8va eg. 1 octave higher than written.

Diatonic 7th Chords in Triplets

Starting on the Root
F min/maj7 arpeggio

Starting on the 2nd
G min7 arpeggio

Starting on the 3rd
Ab maj7/#5 arpeggio

Starting on the 4th
Bb 7#11 arpeggio

Starting on the 5th
C 7 arpeggio

Building a 12 key Facility Pt II

Starting on the 6th
D min7 b5 arpeggio

Starting on the 7th
E min7 b5 arpeggio

Starting on the Root
F min/maj 7 arpeggio

4 Note Groupings Diatonic Triads

Ascending 1351

min   min   aug   maj   maj   dim   dim   min

Descending 1351

min   dim   dim   maj   maj   aug   min   min

Ascending 1531

min   min   aug   maj   maj   dim   dim   min

Descending 1531

min   dim   dim   maj   maj   aug   min   min

4 Note Groupings Diatonic 7th Chords

Ascending

min/maj7 min7   maj7#5   dom7   dom7   half dim7   half dim7   min/maj7

min7   maj7#5   dom7   dom7   half dim7   half dim7   min/maj7

Descending

min/maj7 half dim7 half dim7 dom7   dom7   maj7 #5   min7   min/maj7

half dim7   half dim7 dom7   dom7   maj7 #5   min7   min/maj7

Permutation 2
Ascending & descending

min/maj7 min7   maj7#5   dom7   dom7   half dim7   half dim7   min/maj7

half dim7   half dim7 dom7   dom7   maj7#5   min7   min/maj7

Permutation 3
Down the chord stepwise up the scale

min/maj7   min7   maj7#5   dom7   dom7   half dim7   half dim7   min/maj7

min/maj7   half dim7   half dim7   dom7   dom7   maj7 #5   min7   min/maj7

Scale studies in the key of F# Melodic Minor

Scales, Modes and Arpeggios over 2 octaves

F# Melodic minor scale

F# min maj7 arpeggio

G# sus b9 scale

G# sus b9 arpeggio

A Lydian augmented scale

A maj #5 arpeggio

B Lydian dominant scale

B 7 #11 arpeggio

Building a 12 key Facility Pt II

F# Melodic minor/ C# scale

F# minmaj7 / C# arpeggio

D# Locrian #2 scale

D# min7 b5 arpeggio

E# Altered scale

E# Alt. arpeggio

4 Note Scale Groupings

The following exercise outlines the use of 4 note groupings moving stepwise diatonically through the scale of F# melodic minor.

For example, the 4 note grouping starts on the root note or 1st degree of the scale and progresses stepwise . The exercise then descends from the 2nd octave F# back to the root.

Ascending

Descending

* The D in this exercise is out of the range of the 4 string bass without C extension. This passage can
be played 8va eg. 1 octave higher than written.

Permutation 2   Up & Down

As in the previous exercise the following exercise outlines the use of 4 note groupings moving stepwise diatonically
through the scale of F# melodic minor.
Notice in exercise #2 the 4 note grouping starts on the root note or 1st degree of the scale and progresses stepwise. In
this example we descend when we hit the 5th note in the sequence eg. descending from the 2nd 4 note grouping.

Ascending

Descending

Broken Thirds

Ascending

Descending

3 Note Groupings

F# Melodic minor scale in triplet groupings
Ascending

Descending

Diatonic 7th Chords in Triplets

Starting on the Root
F# min/maj7 arpeggio

Starting on the 2nd
G# min7 arpeggio

Starting on the 3rd
A maj7/#5 arpeggio

Starting on the 4th
B 7#11 arpeggio

Starting on the 5th
C# 7 arpeggio

Starting on the 6th
D# min7 b5 arpeggio

Starting on the 7th
E# min7 b5 arpeggio

Starting on the Root
F# min/maj 7 arpeggio

4 Note Groupings Diatonic Triads

Ascending 1351

| min | min | aug | maj | maj | dim | dim | min |

Descending 1351

| min | dim | dim | maj | maj | aug | min | min |

Ascending 1531

| min | min | aug | maj | maj | dim | dim | min |

Descending 1531

| min | dim | dim | maj | maj | aug | min | min |

4 Note Groupings Diatonic 7th Chords

Ascending

min/maj7 min7   maj7#5   dom7   dom7   half dim7   half dim7   min/maj7

min7   maj7#5   dom7   dom7   half dim7   half dim7   min/maj7

Descending

min/maj7   half dim7   half dim7   dom7   dom7   maj7 #5   min7   min/maj7

half dim7   half dim7   dom7   dom7   maj7 #5   min7   min/maj7

Permutation 2
Ascending & descending

min/maj7 min7   maj7#5   dom7   dom7   half dim7   half dim7   min/maj7

half dim7   half dim7   dom7   dom7   maj7#5   min7   min/maj7

Permutation 3
Down the chord stepwise up the scale

Scale studies in the key of G Melodic Minor

Scales, Modes and Arpeggios over 2 octaves

G Melodic minor scale

G min maj7 arpeggio

A sus b9 scale

A sus b9 arpeggio

Bb Lydian augmented scale

Bb maj #5 arpeggio

C Lydian dominant scale

C 7 #11 arpeggio

G Melodic minor/ D scale

G minmaj7 / D arpeggio

E Locrian #2 scale

E Half dim #2 arpeggio

F# Altered scale

F# Alt. arpeggio

4 Note Scale Groupings

The following exercise outlines the use of 4 note groupings moving stepwise diatonically through the scale of G melodic minor.

For example, the 4 note grouping starts on the root note or 1st degree of the scale and progresses stepwise . The exercise then descends from the 2nd octave G back to the root.

Ascending

Descending

Permutation 2   ## Up & Down

As in the previous exercise the following exercise outlines the use of 4 note groupings moving stepwise diatonically through the scale of G melodic minor.

Notice in exercise #2 the 4 note grouping starts on the root note or 1st degree of the scale and progresses stepwise. In this example we descend when we hit the 5th note in the sequence eg. descending from the 2nd 4 note grouping.

Ascending

Descending

Broken Thirds

Ascending

Descending

3 Note Groupings

G Melodic minor scale in triplet groupings
Ascending

Descending

Diatonic 7th Chords in Triplets

Starting on the Root
G min/maj7 arpeggio

Starting on the 2nd
A min7 arpeggio

Starting on the 3rd
Bb maj7/#5 arpeggio

Starting on the 4th
C 7#11 arpeggio

Starting on the 5th
D 7 arpeggio

Building a 12 key Facility Pt II

Starting on the 6th
E min7 b5 arpeggio

Starting on the 7th
F# min7 b5 arpeggio

Starting on the Root
G min/maj 7 arpeggio

4 Note Groupings Diatonic Triads

Ascending 1351

Descending 1351

Ascending 1531

Descending 1531

4 Note Groupings Diatonic 7th Chords

Ascending

min/maj7 min7   maj7#5   dom7   dom7   half dim7   half dim7   min/maj7

min7   maj7#5   dom7   dom7   half dim7   half dim7   min/maj7

Descending

min/maj7 half dim7 half dim7 dom7   dom7   maj7 #5   min7   min/maj7

half dim7 half dim7 dom7   dom7   maj7 #5   min7   min/maj7

Permutation 2
Ascending & descending

min/maj7 min7   maj7#5   dom7   dom7   half dim7   half dim7   min/maj7

half dim7 half dim7 dom7   dom7   maj7#5   min7   min/maj7

Building a 12 key Facility Pt II

Permutation 3
Down the chord stepwise up the scale

min/maj7 min7   maj7#5   dom7   dom7   half dim7   half dim7 min/maj7

min/maj7 half dim7   half dim7 dom7   dom7   maj7 #5   min7   min/maj7

Scale studies in the key of Ab Melodic Minor

Scales, Modes and Arpeggios over 2 octaves

Ab Melodic minor scale

Ab min maj7 arpeggio

Bb sus b9 scale

Bb sus b9 arpeggio

Cb Lydian augmented scale

Cb maj #5 arpeggio

Db Lydian dominant scale

Db 7 #11 arpeggio

Building a 12 key Facility Pt II

Ab Melodic minor/ Eb scale

Ab minmaj7 / Eb arpeggio

F Locrian #2 scale

F min7 b5 arpeggio

G Altered scale

G Alt. arpeggio

4 Note Scale Groupings

The following exercise outlines the use of 4 note groupings moving stepwise diatonically through the scale of Ab melodic minor

For example, the 4 note grouping starts on the root note or 1st degree of the scale and progresses stepwise . The exercise then descends from the 2nd octave Ab back to the root.

Ascending

Descending

Permutation 2   Up & Down

As in the previous exercise the following exercise outlines the use of 4 note groupings moving stepwise diatonically through the scale of Ab melodic minor.

Notice in exercise #2 the 4 note grouping starts on the root note or 1st degree of the scale and progresses stepwise. In this example we descend when we hit the 5th note in the sequence eg. descending from the 2nd 4 note grouping.

Ascending

Descending

Broken Thirds

Ascending

Descending

3 Note Groupings

Ab Melodic minor scale in triplet groupings
Ascending

Descending

Diatonic 7th Chords in Triplets

Starting on the Root
Ab min/maj7 arpeggio

Starting on the 2nd
Bb min7 arpeggio

Starting on the 3rd
Cb maj7/#5 arpeggio

Starting on the 4th
Db 7#11 arpeggio

Starting on the 5th
Eb 7 arpeggio

Starting on the 6th
F min7 b5 arpeggio

Starting on the 7th
G min7 b5 arpeggio

Starting on the Root
Ab min/maj 7 arpeggio

4 Note Groupings Diatonic Triads

Ascending 1351

min min aug maj maj dim dim min

Descending 1351

min dim dim maj maj aug min min

Ascending 1531

min min aug maj maj dim dim min

Descending 1531

min dim dim maj maj aug min min

4 Note Groupings Diatonic 7th Chords

Ascending

min/maj7   min7   maj7#5   dom7   dom7   half dim7   half dim7   min/maj7

min7   maj7#5   dom7   dom7   half dim7   half dim7   min/maj7

Descending

min/maj7   half dim7   half dim7   dom7   dom7   maj7 #5   min7   min/maj7

half dim7   half dim7   dom7   dom7   maj7 #5   min7   min/maj7

Permutation 2
Ascending & descending

min/maj7   min7   maj7#5   dom7   dom7   half dim7   half dim7   min/maj7

half dim7   half dim7   dom7   dom7   maj7#5   min7   min/maj7

Permutation 3
Down the chord stepwise up the scale

min/maj7 min7   maj7#5   dom7   dom7   half dim7   half dim7   min/maj7

min/maj7   half dim7   half dim7   dom7   dom7   maj7 #5   min7   min/maj7

Scale studies in the key of A Melodic Minor

Scales, Modes and Arpeggios over 2 octaves

A Melodic minor scale

A min maj7 arpeggio

B sus b9 scale

B sus b9 arpeggio

C Lydian augmented scale

C maj #5 arpeggio

D Lydian dominant scale

D 7 #11 arpeggio

A Melodic minor/E scale

A minmaj7 /E arpeggio

F# Locrian #2 scale

F# min7 b5 arpeggio

G# Altered scale

G# Alt. arpeggio

4 Note Scale Groupings

The following exercise outlines the use of 4 note groupings moving stepwise diatonically through the scale of A melodic minor.

For example, the 4 note grouping starts on the root note or 1st degree of the scale and progresses stepwise . The exercise then descends from the 2nd octave A back to the root.

Ascending

Building a 12 key Facility Pt II

Descending

Permutation 2   Up & Down

As in the previous exercise the following exercise outlines the use of 4 note groupings moving stepwise diatonically through the scale of A melodic minor.

Notice in exercise #2 the 4 note grouping starts on the root note or 1st degree of the scale and progresses stepwise. In this example we descend when we hit the 5th note in the sequence eg. descending from the 2nd 4 note grouping.

Ascending

Descending

Broken Thirds

Ascending

Descending

3 Note Groupings

A Melodic minor scale in triplet groupings
Ascending

Descending

Diatonic 7th Chords in Triplets

Starting on the Root
A min/maj7 arpeggio

Starting on the 2nd
B min7 arpeggio

Starting on the 3rd
C maj7/#5 arpeggio

Starting on the 4th
D 7#11 arpeggio

Starting on the 5th
E 7 arpeggio

Building a 12 key Facility Pt II

Starting on the 6th
F# min7 b5 arpeggio

Starting on the 7th
G# min7 b5 arpeggio

Starting on the Root
A min/maj 7 arpeggio

4 Note Groupings Diatonic Triads

Ascending 1351

min   min   aug   maj   maj   dim   dim   min

Descending 1351

min   dim   dim   maj   maj   aug   min   min

Ascending 1531

min   min   aug   maj   maj   dim   dim   min

Descending 1531

min   dim   dim   maj   maj   aug   min   min

4 Note Groupings Diatonic 7th Chords

Ascending

min/maj7 min7   maj7#5   dom7   dom7   half dim7   half dim7   min/maj7

min7   maj7#5   dom7   dom7   half dim7   half dim7   min/maj7

Descending

min/maj7   half dim7   half dim7   dom7   dom7   maj7 #5   min7   min/maj7

half dim7   half dim7   dom7   dom7   maj7 #5   min7   min/maj7

Permutation 2
Ascending & descending

min/maj7 min7   maj7#5   dom7   dom7   half dim7   half dim7   min/maj7

half dim7   half dim7   dom7   dom7   maj7#5   min7   min/maj7

Permutation 3
Down the chord stepwise up the scale

min/maj7 min7   maj7#5   dom7   dom7   half dim7   half dim7   min/maj7

min/maj7 half dim7 half dim7 dom7   dom7   maj7 #5   min7   min/maj7

Scale studies in the key of Bb Melodic Minor

Scales, Modes and Arpeggios over 2 octaves

Bb Melodic minor scale

Bb min maj7 arpeggio

C sus b9 scale

C sus b9 arpeggio

Db Lydian augmented scale

Db maj #5 arpeggio

Eb Lydian dominant scale

Eb 7 #11 arpeggio

Building a 12 key Facility Pt II

Bb Melodic minor/ F scale

Bb minmaj7 /F arpeggio

G Locrian #2 scale

G min7 b5 arpeggio

A Altered scale

A Alt. arpeggio

4 Note Scale Groupings

The following exercise outlines the use of 4 note groupings moving stepwise diatonically through the scale of Bb melodic minor.

For example, the 4 note grouping starts on the root note or 1st degree of the scale and progresses stepwise . The exercise then descends from the 2nd octave Bb back to the root.

Ascending

Descending

Permutation 2   Up & Down

As in the previous exercise the following exercise outlines the use of 4 note groupings moving stepwise diatonically through the scale of Bb melodic minor.

Notice in exercise #2 the 4 note grouping starts on the root note or 1st degree of the scale and progresses stepwise. In this example we descend when we hit the 5th note in the sequence eg. descending from the 2nd 4 note grouping.

Ascending

Descending

Broken Thirds

Ascending

Descending

3 Note Groupings

Bb Melodic minor scale in triplet groupings
Ascending

Descending

Diatonic 7th Chords in Triplets

Starting on the Root
Bb min/maj7 arpeggio

Starting on the 2nd
C min7 arpeggio

Starting on the 3rd
Db maj7/#5 arpeggio

Starting on the 4th
Eb 7#11 arpeggio

Starting on the 5th
F 7 arpeggio

Starting on the 6th
G min7 b5 arpeggio

Starting on the 7th
A min7 b5 arpeggio

Starting on the Root
Bb min/maj 7 arpeggio

4 Note Groupings Diatonic Triads

Ascending 1351

min   min   aug   maj   maj   dim   dim   min

Descending 1351

min   dim   dim   maj   maj   aug   min   min

Ascending 1531

min   min   aug   maj   maj   dim   dim   min

Descending 1531

min   dim   dim   maj   maj   aug   min   min

4 Note Groupings Diatonic 7th Chords

Ascending

min/maj7 min7   maj7#5   dom7   dom7   half dim7   half dim7   min/maj7

min7   maj7#5   dom7   dom7   half dim7   half dim7   min/maj7

Descending

min/maj7   half dim7   half dim7   dom7   dom7   maj7 #5   min7   min/maj7

half dim7   half dim7   dom7   dom7   maj7 #5   min7   min/maj7

Permutation 2
Ascending & descending

min/maj7 min7   maj7#5   dom7   dom7   half dim7   half dim7   min/maj7

half dim7   half dim7   dom7   dom7   maj7#5   min7   min/maj7

Permutation 3
Down the chord stepwise up the scale

Scale studies in the key of B Melodic Minor

Scales, Modes and Arpeggios over 2 octaves

B Melodic minor scale

B min maj7 arpeggio

C# sus b9 scale

C# sus b9 arpeggio

D Lydian augmented scale

D maj #5 arpeggio

E Lydian dominant scale

E 7 #11 arpeggio

C# Melodic minor/ F# scale

C# minmaj7 / F# arpeggio

G# Locrian #2 scale

G# min7 b5 arpeggio

A# Altered scale

A# Alt. arpeggio

4 Note Scale Groupings

The following exercise outlines the use of 4 note groupings moving stepwise diatonically through the scale of B melodic minor.

For example, the 4 note grouping starts on the root note or 1st degree of the scale and progresses stepwise . The exercise then descends from the 2nd octave B back to the root.

Ascending

Descending

Permutation 2   Up & Down

As in the previous exercise the following exercise outlines the use of 4 note groupings moving stepwise diatonically through the scale of B melodic minor.

Notice in exercise #2 the 4 note grouping starts on the root note or 1st degree of the scale and progresses stepwise. In this example we descend when we hit the 5th note in the sequence eg. descending from the 2nd 4 note grouping.

Ascending

Descending

Broken Thirds

Ascending

Descending

3 Note Groupings

B Melodic minor scale in triplet groupings
Ascending

Descending

Diatonic 7th Chords in Triplets

Starting on the Root
B min/maj7 arpeggio

Starting on the 2nd
C# min7 arpeggio

Starting on the 3rd
D maj7/#5 arpeggio

Starting on the 4th
E 7#11 arpeggio

Starting on the 5th
F# 7 arpeggio

Building a 12 key Facility Pt II

Starting on the 6th
G# min7 b5 arpeggio

Starting on the 7th
A# min7 b5 arpeggio

Starting on the Root
B min/maj 7 arpeggio

4 Note Groupings Diatonic Triads

Ascending 1351

min   min   aug   maj   maj   dim   dim   min

Descending 1351

min   dim   dim   maj   maj   aug   min   min

Ascending 1531

min   min   aug   maj   maj   dim   dim   min

Descending 1531

min   dim   dim   maj   maj   aug   min   min

4 Note Groupings Diatonic 7th Chords

Ascending

min/maj7 min7 maj7#5 dom7 dom7 half dim7 half dim7 min/maj7

min7 maj7#5 dom7 dom7 half dim7 half dim7 min/maj7

Descending

min/maj7 half dim7 half dim7 dom7 dom7 maj7 #5 min7 min/maj7

half dim7 half dim7 dom7 dom7 maj7 #5 min7 min/maj7

Permutation 2
Ascending & descending

min/maj7 min7 maj7#5 dom7 dom7 half dim7 half dim7 min/maj7

half dim7 half dim7 dom7 dom7 maj7#5 min7 min/maj7

Building a 12 key Facility Pt II

Permutation 3
Down the chord stepwise up the scale

Part III   The Symmetric Scales

The whole tone scale consists of a series of whole steps or tones. Due to the consistant pattern of intervals it is refered to as a symmetric scale.

As a result of the whole step formula there are only two whole tone scales, all other whole tone scales are derived from these.

For the purpose of this book we are using the C whole tone scale and the Db whole tone scale to illustrate the examples.

The Whole tone scales

C Whole tone scale

Db whole tone scale

4 Note Scale Groupings

The following exercise outlines the use of 4 note groupings moving stepwise diatonically through the C whole tone scale. For example, the 4 note grouping starts on the root note or 1st degree of the scale andprogresses stepwise . The exercise then descends from the 2nd octave C back to the root.

Ascending

Descending

Permutation 2   Up & Down

As in the previous exercise the following exercise outlines the use of 4 note groupings moving stepwise diatonically through the C whole tone scale.

Notice in exercise #2 the 4 note grouping starts on the root note or 1st degree of the scale and progresses stepwise. In this example we descend when we hit the 5th note in the sequence eg. descending from the 2nd 4 note grouping.

Ascending

Descending

Broken Thirds

Ascending

Descending

3 Note Groupings

C Whole tone scale in triplets
Ascending

Descending

C Whole tone Diatonic Triads
Ascending

Descending

4 Note Groupings Diatonic Triads

Ascending 1351

Descending 1351

Building a 12 key Facility Pt II

Ascending 1531

Descending 1531

4 Note Groupings Diatonic 7th Chords

Ascending

Permutation 2
Ascending & descending

Permutation 3
Down the chord stepwise up the scale

Db Whole Tone Scale

Db whole tone scale

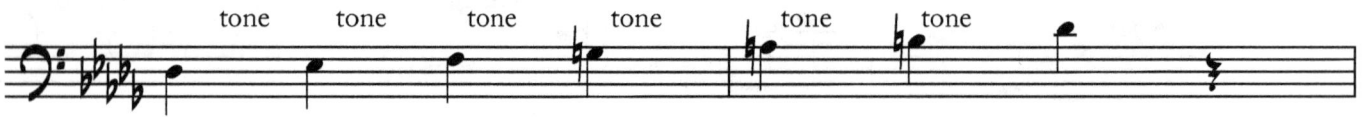

4 Note Scale Groupings

The following exercise outlines the use of 4 note groupings moving stepwise diatonically through the Db whole tone scale. For example, the 4 note grouping starts on the root note or 1st degree of the scale and progresses stepwise . The exercise then descends from the 2nd octave Db back to the root.

Ascending

Descending

Permutation 2 — Up & Down

As in the previous exercise the following exercise outlines the use of 4 note groupings moving stepwise diatonically through the Db whole tone scale.

Notice in exercise #2 the 4 note grouping starts on the root note or 1st degree of the scale and progresses stepwise. In this example we descend when we hit the 5th note in the sequence eg. descending from the 2nd 4 note grouping.

Ascending

Descending

Broken Thirds

Ascending

Descending

3 Note Groupings

Db Whole tone scale in triplets
Ascending

Descending

Db whole tone Diatonic triads
Ascending

Descending

4 Note Groupings Diatonic Triads

Ascending 1351

Descending 1351

Ascending 1531

4 Note Groupings Diatonic 7th Chords

Descending 1531

Ascending

Descending

Permutation 2
Ascending & descending

Building a 12 key Facility Pt II

Permutation 3
Down the chord stepwise up the scale

The Diminished Scale (whole half step)

The diminished scale shown below is another of the symmetric scales.
The formula of intervals is whole step, half step or tone, semi tone.
Due to the symmetrical nature of the scale there are only 3 diminished scales, all other scales are built from these 3 scales.
For the purpose of this book we are using the C, Db and D diminished scale to illustrate the examples.

4 Note Scale Groupings

The following exercise outlines the use of 4 note groupings moving stepwise diatonically through the C diminished scale.
For example, the 4 note grouping starts on the root note or 1st degree of the scale and
progresses stepwise . The exercise then descends from the 2nd octave C back to the root.

Ascending

Descending

Permutation 2

Up & Down

As in the previous exercise the following exercise outlines the use of 4 note groupings moving stepwise diatonically through the C diminished scale.

Notice in exercise #2 the 4 note grouping starts on the root note or 1st degree of the scale and progresses stepwise. In this example we descend when we hit the 5th note in the sequence eg. descending from the 2nd 4 note grouping.

Ascending

Descending

Broken Thirds

Ascending

Descending

3 Note Groupings

C diminished scale in triplets
Ascending

Descending

C Diminished Scale Diatonic Triads

Ascending 135

Descending 153

4 Note Groupings Diatonic Triads

Ascending 1351

Descending 1351

Ascending 1531

Descending 1531

4 Note Groupings Diatonic 7th Chords

Ascending

Descending

Permutation 2
Ascending & descending

Permutation 3
Down the chord stepwise up the scale

The Db Diminished Scale (whole half step)

4 Note Scale Groupings

The following exercise outlines the use of 4 note groupings moving stepwise diatonically through the Db diminished scale.

For example, the 4 note grouping starts on the root note or 1st degree of the scale and progresses stepwise . The exercise then descends from the 2nd octave Db back to the root.

Ascending

Descending

Permutation 2   Up & Down

As in the previous exercise the following exercise outlines the use of 4 note groupings moving stepwise diatonically through the Db diminished scale.

Notice in exercise #2 the 4 note grouping starts on the root note or 1st degree of the scale and progresses stepwise. In this example we descend when we hit the 5th note in the sequence eg. descending from the 2nd 4 note grouping.

Ascending

Descending

Broken Thirds

Ascending

Descending

3 Note Groupings

Db diminished scale in triplets
Ascending

Descending

Db Diminished Scale Diatonic Triads

Ascending 135

Descending 153

4 Note Groupings Diatonic Triads

Ascending 1351

Descending 1351

Ascending 1531

Descending 1531

4 Note Groupings Diatonic 7th Chords

Ascending

Descending

Building a 12 key Facility Pt II

Permutation 2
Ascending & descending

Permutation 3
Down the chord stepwise up the scale

The D Diminished Scale (whole half step)

tone   semi tone   tone   semi tone   tone   semi tone   tone   semi tone

4 Note Scale Groupings

The following exercise outlines the use of 4 note groupings moving stepwise diatonically through the D diminished scale. For example, the 4 note grouping starts on the root note or 1st degree of the scale and progresses stepwise . The exercise then descends from the 2nd octave D back to the root.

Ascending

Descending

Permutation 2   Up & Down

As in the previous exercise the following exercise outlines the use of 4 note groupings moving stepwise diatonically through the D Diminished scale.

Notice in exercise #2 the 4 note grouping starts on the root note or 1st degree of the scale and progresses stepwise. In this example we descend when we hit the 5th note in the sequence eg. descending from the 2nd 4 note grouping.

Ascending

Descending

Broken Thirds

Ascending

Descending

3 Note Groupings

D diminished scale in triplets
Ascending

Descending

D Diminished Scale Diatonic Triads

Ascending 135

Descending 153

4 Note Groupings Diatonic Triads

Ascending 1351

Descending 1351

Ascending 1531

Descending 1531

4 Note Groupings Diatonic 7th Chords

Ascending

Descending

Permutation 2
Ascending & descending

Permutation 3
Down the chord stepwise up the scale

The C Diminished Scale (half whole step)

The half whole diminished scale is made up of the half step (semi tone) whole step (tone) formula.
Like the whole step, half step diminished scale due to its symmetric construction there are only 3 scales, all others are derived from these. For the purpose of this book we will be using C, Db and D to outline the diminished exercises.

4 Note Scale Groupings

The following exercise outlines the use of 4 note groupings moving stepwise diatonically through the C half whole diminished scale.
For example, the 4 note grouping starts on the root note or 1st degree of the scale and progresses stepwise . The exercise then descends from the 2nd octave C back to the root.

Ascending

Descending

Permutation 2   Up & Down

As in the previous exercise the following exercise outlines the use of 4 note groupings moving stepwise diatonically through the C half whole diminished scale.

Notice in exercise #2 the 4 note grouping starts on the root note or 1st degree of the scale and progresses stepwise. In this example we descend when we hit the 5th note in the sequence eg. descending from the 2nd 4 note grouping.

Ascending

Descending

Broken Thirds

Ascending

Descending

3 Note Groupings

C half whole diminished scale in triplets
Ascending

Descending

C Half Whole Diminished Scale Diatonic Triads

Ascending 135

Descending 153

4 Note Groupings Diatonic Triads

Ascending 1351

Descending 1351

Ascending 1531

Descending 1531

4 Note Groupings Diatonic 7th Chords

Ascending

Descending

Permutation 2
Ascending & descending

Permutation 3
Down the chord stepwise up the scale

The Db Diminished Scale (half whole step)

semi tone   tone   semi tone   tone   semi tone   tone   semi tone   tone

4 Note Scale Groupings

The following exercise outlines the use of 4 note groupings moving stepwise diatonically through the Db half whole diminished scale.

For example, the 4 note grouping starts on the root note or 1st degree of the scale and progresses stepwise . The exercise then descends from the 2nd octave Db back to the root.

Ascending

Descending

Permutation 2   Up & Down

As in the previous exercise the following exercise outlines the use of 4 note groupings moving stepwise diatonically through the Db half whole diminished scale.

Notice in exercise #2 the 4 note grouping starts on the root note or 1st degree of the scale and progresses stepwise. In this example we descend when we hit the 5th note in the sequence eg. descending from the 2nd 4 note grouping.

Ascending

Descending

Broken Thirds

Ascending

Descending

3 Note Groupings

Db half whole diminished scale in triplets
Ascending

Descending

Db Half Whole Diminished Scale Diatonic Triads

Ascending 135

Descending 153

4 Note Groupings Diatonic Triads

Ascending 1351

dim dim dim dim dim dim dim dim dim

Descending 1351

dim dim dim dim dim dim dim dim dim

Ascending 1531

dim dim dim dim dim dim dim dim dim

Descending 1531

dim dim dim dim dim dim dim dim dim

4 Note Groupings Diatonic 7th Chords

Ascending

dim dim dim dim dim dim dim dim dim

Descending

dim dim dim dim dim dim dim dim dim

213

Permutation 2
Ascending & descending

Permutation 3
Down the chord stepwise up the scale

The D Diminished Scale (half whole step)

semi tone　　tone　　semi tone　　tone　　semi tone　　tone　　semi tone　　tone

4 Note Scale Groupings

The following exercise outlines the use of 4 note groupings moving stepwise diatonically through the D half whole diminished scale.

For example, the 4 note grouping starts on the root note or 1st degree of the scale and progresses stepwise . The exercise then descends from the 2nd octave D back to the root.

Ascending

Descending

Permutation 2   Up & Down

As in the previous exercise the following exercise outlines the use of 4 note groupings moving stepwise diatonically through the D half whole diminished scale.

Notice in exercise #2 the 4 note grouping starts on the root note or 1st degree of the scale and progresses stepwise. In this example we descend when we hit the 5th note in the sequence eg. descending from the 2nd 4 note grouping.

Ascending

Descending

Broken Thirds

Ascending

Descending

3 Note Groupings

D half whole diminished scale in triplets
Ascending

Descending

D Half Whole Diminished Scale Diatonic Triads

Ascending 135

Descending 153

4 Note Groupings Diatonic Triads

Ascending 1351

dim   dim   dim   dim   dim   dim   dim   dim   dim

Descending 1351

dim   dim   dim   dim   dim   dim   dim   dim   dim

Ascending 1531

dim   dim   dim   dim   dim   dim   dim   dim   dim

Descending 1531

dim   dim   dim   dim   dim   dim   dim   dim   dim

4 Note Groupings Diatonic 7th Chords

Ascending

dim   dim   dim   dim   dim   dim   dim   dim   dim

Descending

dim   dim   dim   dim   dim   dim   dim   dim   dim

Building a 12 key Facility Pt II

Permutation 2
Ascending & descending

Permutation 3
Down the chord stepwise up the scale

THE AUGMENTED SCALE

The Augmented scale is another of the symmetric scales and consists of a min 3rd followed by a 1/2 step or semi tone.
It can also be thought of as 2 augmented triads a 1/2 step away. eg . in the key of C a B aug triad and C aug triad.

Due to the symmetric construction of the augmented scale there are 4 scales, all others are derived from these scales.
For the purpose of this book we will use C, Db,D and Eb to outline the augmented scale exercises.

C Augmented Scale

* Note the D# and Eb and G# and Ab are enharmonically the same note.

C Augmented scale in triplets
Ascending

Descending

C Augmented triads
Ascending the C Aug triad Descending down the B Aug triad resolving to the root C

C Augmented Diatonic 7th chords
Ascending

Cmaj7#5   Emaj7#5   Ab maj7#5   Cmaj7#5

Descending

Cmaj7#5   Abmaj7#5   Emaj7#5   Cmaj7#5

Db Augmented Scale

min 3rd   semi tone   min3rd   semi tone   min 3rd   semi tone

C aug triad   Db Aug triad

Db Augmented scale in triplets
Ascending

Descending

Db Augmented triads
Ascending the Db Aug triad Descending down the C Aug triad resolving to the root Db

Db Aug triad   C Aug triad

Db Augmented Diatonic 7th chords
Ascending

Db maj7#5   F maj7#5   A maj7#5   Db maj7#5

Descending
Db maj7#5   A maj7#5   F maj7#5   Db maj7#5

D Augmented Scale

min 3rd   semi tone   min3rd   semi tone   min 3rd   semi tone

C# Aug triad   D Aug triad

Note that the E# is the same note as F natural & the A# is the same note as Bb

D Augmented scale in triplets
Ascending

Descending

D Augmented triads
Ascending the D Aug triad Descending down the C# Aug triad resolving to the root D

D Aug triad   C# Aug triad

D Augmented Diatonic 7th chords
Ascending

D maj7#5   F# maj7#5   Bb maj7#5   D maj7#5

Descending
D maj7#5   Bb maj7#5   F# maj7#5   D maj7#5

* Note that the E# is the same note as F natural & the A# is the same note as Bb

Eb Augmented Scale

min 3rd semi tone min3rd semi tone min 3rd semi tone

D Aug triad

Eb Aug triad

Eb Augmented scale in triplets
Ascending

Descending

Eb Augmented triads
Ascending the Eb Aug triad Descending down the D Aug triad resolving to the root Eb

Eb Aug triad

D Aug triad

Eb Augmented Diatonic 7th chords
Ascending

Eb maj7#5   G maj7#5   B maj7#5   Eb maj7#5

Descending
Eb maj7#5   B maj7#5   G maj7#5   Eb maj7#5

Part IV.   The Major BeBop Scale

The bebop scales are similar to there parent scales in this case the Major scale.
The difference between the scales is the additional chromatic passing tone in the bebop scale.

By adding the chromatic passisng tone between the 5th and 6th degree of the scale the chord tones remain on the downbeats giving the scale a stronger sense of forward motion.

By looking at the examples below the chord tones remain on the downbeats in the bebop scale. When looking at the second octave of the major scale the chord tones are no longer on the downbeats eg. 1 & 3.

Major Bebop scale

* Indicates the chromatic passing tone Ab in the key of C or the b6th of the scale

The Major scale

The Major BEBOP scales in 12 keys

C Major Bebop scale ascending

C Major Bebop scale descending

C.T = chord tone

Db Major Bebop scale ascending

Db Major Bebop scale descending

D Major Bebop scale ascending

D Major Bebop scale descending

Eb Major Bebop scale ascending

Eb Major Bebop scale descending

E Major Bebop scale ascending

E Major Bebop scale descending

F Major Bebop scale ascending

F Major Bebop scale descending

F# Major Bebop scale ascending

F# Major Bebop scale descending

G Major Bebop scale ascending

G Major Bebop scale descending

Ab Major Bebop scale ascending

Ab Major Bebop scale descending

A Major Bebop scale ascending

A Major Bebop scale descending

Bb Major Bebop scale ascending

Bb Major Bebop scale descending

B Major Bebop scale ascending

B Major Bebop scale descending

The Dominant 7th BeBop Scale

The bebop scales are similar to there parent scales in this case the Dominant 7th scale.
The difference between the scales is the additional chromatic passing tone in the bebop scale.

By adding the chromatic passisng tone between the b7th and the root note of the scale the chord tones remain on the downbeats giving the scale a stronger sense of forward motion.

By looking at the examples below the chord tones remain on the downbeats in the bebop scale. When looking at the second octave of the Dominant scale the chord tones are no longer on the downbeats eg. 1 & 3.

Dominant Bebop scale

* Indicates the chromatic passing tone B natural in the key of C or the major 7th of the scale

The Dominant scale

The Dominant BEBOP scales in 12 keys

C Dominant Bebop scale ascending

C Dominant Bebop scale descending

Db Dominant Bebop scale ascending

Db Dominant Bebop scale descending

D Dominant Bebop scale ascending

D Dominant Bebop scale descending

Eb Dominant Bebop scale ascending

Eb Dominant Bebop scale descending

E Dominant Bebop scale ascending

E Dominant Bebop scale descending

F Dominant Bebop scale ascending

F Dominant Bebop scale descending

F# Dominant Bebop scale ascending

F# Dominant Bebop scale descending

G Dominant Bebop scale ascending

G Dominant Bebop scale descending

Ab Dominant Bebop scale ascending

Ab Dominant Bebop scale descending

A Dominant Bebop scale ascending

A Dominant Bebop scale descending

Bb Dominant Bebop scale ascending

Bb Dominant Bebop scale descending

B Dominant Bebop scale ascending

B Dominant Bebop scale descending

The Minor Be Bop Scale

The bebop scales are similar to there parent scales in this case the Dorian Minor scale.
The difference between the scales is the additional chromatic passing tone in the bebop scale.

By adding the chromatic passisng tone between the b7th and the root note of the scale the chord tones remain on the downbeats giving the scale a stronger sense of forward motion.

By looking at the examples below the chord tones remain on the downbeats in the bebop scale. When looking at the second octave of the Dorian Minor scale the chord tones are no longer on the downbeats.

Minor Bebop scale

* Indicates the chromatic passing tone B natural in the key of C or the major 7th of the scale

The Dorian Minor scale

The Minor BeBop scales in 12 keys

C Minor Bebop scale ascending

C Minor Bebop scale descending

C.T = chord tone

C# Minor Bebop scale ascending

C# Minor Bebop scale descending

D Minor Bebop scale ascending

D Minor Bebop scale descending

Eb Minor Bebop scale ascending

Eb Minor Bebop scale descending

E Minor Bebop scale ascending

E Minor Bebop scale descending

F Minor Bebop scale ascending

F Minor Bebop scale descending

F# Minor Bebop scale ascending

F# Minor Bebop scale descending

G Minor Bebop scale ascending

G Minor Bebop scale descending

G# Minor Bebop scale ascending

G# Minor Bebop scale descending

A Minor Bebop scale ascending

A Minor Bebop scale descending

Bb Minor Bebop scale ascending

Bb Minor Bebop scale descending

B Minor Bebop scale ascending

B Minor Bebop scale descending

Part V   The Blues Scale

The Blues scale is one of the most commonly used scales for the jazz and rock and blues musicians.
The scale construction is 1 b3 4 b5 5 b7.

The examples below outline the Blues scale in all 12 keys.

C Blues scale ascending

C Blues scale descending

Db Blues scale ascending

Db Blues scale descending

D Blues scale ascending

D Blues scale descending

Eb Blues scale ascending

Eb Blues scale descending

E Blues scale ascending

E Blues scale descending

F Blues scale ascending

F Blues scale descending

F# Blues scale ascending

F# Blues scale descending

G Blues scale ascending

G Blues scale descending

Ab Blues scale ascending

Ab Blues scale descending

A Blues scale ascending

A Blues scale descending

Bb Blues scale ascending

Bb Blues scale descending

B Blues scale ascending

B Blues scale descending

Part VI   The Major Pentatonic Scale

The pentatonic scales consist of 5 notes hence the term pentatonic.
Due to the nature of the 5 note construction there are many pentatonic scales used worldwide.
For the the purpose of this chapter we will be looking at the Major pentatonic scale which consists of the notes 1 2 3 5 6 of the major scale.

The Major Pentatonic scale in 12 keys

C major pentatonic ascending

C major pentatonic descending

Db major pentatonic ascending

Db major pentatonic descending

D major pentatonic ascending

D major pentatonic descending

Eb major pentatonic ascending

Eb major pentatonic descending

E major pentatonic ascending

E major pentatonic descending

F major pentatonic ascending

F major pentatonic descending

F# major pentatonic ascending

F# major pentatonic descending

G major pentatonic ascending

G major pentatonic descending

Ab major pentatonic ascending

Ab major pentatonic descending

A major pentatonic ascending

A major pentatonic descending

Bb major pentatonic ascending

Bb major pentatonic descending

B major pentatonic ascending

B major pentatonic descending

The Minor Pentatonic Scales

The minor pentatonic scale is related to the major pentatonic scale eg the relative minor relationship.
As an example the A minor pentatonic scale consists of the same notes as the C major pentatonic scale.
With A minor being the relative minor to C major.
The minor pentatonic scale consists of the root b3 4 5 b7.

The A Minor pentatonic scale.

Ascending

A minor pentatonic scale descending

By reviewing the C major pentatonic scale from the previous chapter shown below, the A minor pentatonic uses the same notes starting on A the relative minor of C major.

C major pentatonic ascending

The Minor Pentatonic in 12 keys

C minor pentatonic ascending

C minor pentatonic scale descending

C# minor pentatonic ascending

C# minor pentatonic descending

D minor pentatonic ascending

D minor pentatonic descending

Eb minor pentatonic ascending

Eb minor pentatonic descending

E minor pentatonic ascending

E minor pentatonic descending

F minor pentatonic ascending

F minor pentatonic descending

F# minor pentatonic ascending

F# minor pentatonic descending

G minor pentatonic ascending

G minor pentatonic descending

G# minor pentatonic ascending

G# minor pentatonic descending

A minor pentatonic ascending

A minor pentatonic descending

Bb minor pentatonic ascending

Bb minor pentatonic descending

B minor pentatonic ascending

B minor pentatonic descending

Part VII   The Harmonic Minor Scale

The harmonic minor scale has a distinctive sound due to the minor 3rd interval between the 6th and 7th degrees of the scale.

The harmonic minor scale is similar to the ascending melodic minor scale with the difference being the b6th degree which creates the minor 3rd interval between the major 7th of the scale.

Harmonic minor scale

Melodic minor scale

* Notice the similarities between the scales with the difference being the 6th degree of the scale, the harmonic minor has a semi tone interval between the 5th and 6th degrees of the scale which creates the minor 3rd interval between the 6th and 7th degrees of the scale.

The Harmonic Minor Scale in 12 keys

C harmonic minor ascending

C harmonic minor descending

C# harmonic minor ascending

C# harmonic minor descending

D harmonic minor ascending

D harmonic minor descending

Eb harmonic minor ascending

Eb harmonic minor descending

E harmonic minor ascending

E harmonic minor descending

F harmonic minor ascending

F harmonic minor descending

F# harmonic minor ascending

F# harmonic minor descending

G harmonic minor ascending

G harmonic minor descending

Ab harmonic minor ascending

Ab harmonic minor descending

A harmonic minor ascending

A harmonic minor descending

Bb harmonic minor ascending

Bb harmonic minor descending

B harmonic minor ascending

B harmonic minor descending

IN CONCLUSION ......

It has been a vast amount of work and dedicated practice that brings the bassist to the last page of this book having covered all the examples within.

It has been the aim of the " Building a 12 key Facility for the Jazz Bassist " book series to give the aspiring bassist a solid grounding in how to practice in 12 keys and develop a dedicated daily practice routine.

Having covered the material in this book you are now well on your way to finding your own voice as a bassist and as a jazz musician.
Listen to as much music as you can, Listen to the masters.

NB. This book is designed to make the student familiar with reading and understanding chord symbols in a jazz context, therefore the use of enharmonics is applied.

The objective has been to make the material for the student as easy to absorb as possible, as a confidance building mechanism.

Your thoughts and comments are important to us and assist us in providing future generations of musicians with quality educational material.

Please send youre thoughts or comments to constructwalkingjazzbasslines@gmail.com

Other books available in this series

PRINT EDITIONS

" Constructing Walking Jazz Bass Lines " Book I
Walking Bass Lines : The Blues in 12 Keys

" Constructing Walking Jazz Bass Lines " Book II
Walking Bass Lines : Rhythm Changes in 12 keys

" Constructing Walking Jazz Bass Lines " Book III
Walking Bass Lines : Standard Lines

" Constructing Walking Jazz Bass Lines " Book IV
Building a 12 Key Facility for the Jazz Bassist Book I

" Constructing Walking Jazz Bass Lines " Book V
Building a 12 Key Facility for the Jazz Bassist Book II

Bass Tablature Series

" Constructing Walking Jazz Bass Lines " Book I
Walking Bass Lines : The Blues in 12 Keys -Bass TAB Edition

" Constructing Walking Jazz Bass Lines " Book II
Walking Bass Lines : Rhythm Changes in 12 Keys - Bass TAB Edition

" Constructing Walking Jazz Bass Lines " Book III
Walking Bass Lines : Standard Lines - Bass TAB Edition

" Constructing Walking Jazz Bass Lines " Book IV
Building a 12 Key Facility for the Jazz Bassist Book I - Bass Tab Edition

"Daily Warm up exercises for Bass Guitar "

E-BOOK EDITIONS

All books in the Constructing Walking Jazz Bass Lines series are also available as an eBook for the following reader formats Kindle, iTunes iBookstore, Nook, and Adobe Digital PDF. Follow us on the web for news and new release updates.

http://waterfallpublishinghouse.com

http://constructingwalkingjazzbasslines.com

http://basstab.net

Waterfall Publishing House is proud to be associated with the Trees for the Future Organisation. Visit them on the web at www.plant-trees.org .
Waterfall Publishing House will plant 1 tree per book sold in the " Constructing Walking Jazz Bass Lines " series through the " Trees for the Future " tree planting program and will match the commitment for a total of 2 trees planted per book sold.

Follow our quarterly progress at Waterfallpublishinghouse.com

www.ingramcontent.com/pod-product-compliance
Lightning Source LLC
Chambersburg PA
CBHW050458110426
42742CB00018B/3299